Essential Read-Spell

Fred J. Schonell

F. Eleanor Schonell

1
Word fun

Illustrated by Malcolm Stokes

GW00726143

Nelson

Contents

The man and the ant 4

Spot and Blot 6

Tom's calf 8

Blot cuts his leg 10

Blot and Ann go for a walk 12

The pig and the mouse 14

The cook and the mice 16

The lost ball 18

The king who was lost 20

Springtime in Switzerland 22

After school 24

The fox and the grapes 26

A party game 28

A picnic by the sea 30

Straw men 32

Monkey and crocodile 34

The best game 36

The king and the page boy 38
The white rabbit 40
The ice boat 42
My school 44
Hay time 46
On the farm 48
Tony, the clever seal 50
The wind and the rain 52
Summer or winter? 54
Little black duck 56
Ritsie and her kittens 58
Whiskers 60
The Christmas tree 1 62
The Christmas tree 2 64
The Christmas tree 3 66
The Christmas tree 4 68

man	met	fun
can	get	run
ran	wet	gun
ant	let	sun

The man and the ant

One day a man with a gun was going down
the road when he met an ant.

The poor ant had hurt his leg
and was lying on the wet road.

He had been run over by a car.

The man stopped and put his gun down on the road.

"Can I help you?" he said.

"Oh, yes, please," said the ant.
"A car ran over my leg."

"Well," said the man, "get on to my cap
and I will let you stop in the sun to dry."

"Oh, this is fun," said the ant.

"I will soon get well up here, in the sun.

Thank you very much, Mr Man."

5   **A**   Write out the sentences, putting in the missing words.

1   The man met an . . .
2   The man had a . . .
3   The poor ant was run over by a . . .
4   You can sit there and dry in the . . .

B   1   Write *three* words that rhyme with *get*.
2   Write *three* words that rhyme with *fun*.
3   Write *three* words that rhyme with *can*.

C   Yes–No Fun. Write 'Yes' or 'No' to these sentences.

1   Can a gun run?
2   Was the ant wet?
3   Is the sun hot?
4   Did the ant get in the man's shoe?

6

red	did	hot
bed	hid	not
fed	lid	blot
led	lip	spot

Spot and Blot

Ann had two little dogs.
They were called 'Spot' and 'Blot'.

Spot had a big white spot on his back,
so Ann called him Spot.

Blot had a big black patch like a blot of ink
on his nose and his lip.
So Ann called this dog Blot .

Spot had a red nose.
Blot had a black nose.

Ann fed them from a big saucepan lid.

One day Ann fed Spot but could not find Blot.

He ran away and hid under her bed,
so he did not get his dinner hot.

Each night Ann led the dogs to a box to sleep.

A Write the words in each line that have the *last two letters* like the one in the box.

red	bed	hid	led	fed	lip
not	hot	hat	net	pot	blot
hid	did	bed	led	lid	kid

B Write the sentences, putting in the correct words.
1 Blot had a black patch on his . . . (leg, lip, foot).
2 Blot hid under a . . . (lid, bed, box).
3 The mark on Spot's back was . . . (white, black, red).

C Write *three* words that have -ot in them.

had	bud	tell
sad	mud	fell
glad	rug	bell
has	dug	well

Tom's calf

Tom's father has a farm.

One day he said,
"Dad, may I have a calf of my own?
I would be so glad if I had a calf."

"Well," said his father,
"you can have the next calf that is born."

Tom now has a calf.

It has a coat of gold and brown like a rose bud.

It is as soft as a rug.

Around its neck is a little bell to tell Tom where it is.

One day the calf fell in the mud in a hole
that Tom had dug.

The mother cow was sad to see her calf in the mud.

A Write on your paper the word left out of each sentence (mud, dug, rug).

1 Tom's calf has a coat as soft as a . . .
2 The calf fell in the . . .
3 Tom had . . . a hole.

B 1 Write *three* words that rhyme with *had*.
2 Write *three* words that rhyme with *tell*.
3 Write *three* words that rhyme with *can*.

C Make little drawings of these:
the calf   the bell   a rug
the hole that Tom dug   a rose bud
Write the names underneath them.

pin	pet	top
tin	set	stop
win	leg	shop
tip	peg	dog

Blot cuts his leg

One day Ann said to her pet dog, "I'll race you to the shop. Come on. Get ready. Go."

Blot ran very fast.

"You win," cried Ann.

Ann had to buy some pins at the shop for her mother.

On the way home Blot cut his leg on a tin.

"Stop, Blot, stop," cried Ann. "I will carry you home."

When she got home Mother said,
"We will tip some warm water
on top of the cut and that will
make it better.

Now we will tie Blot to his peg so that
he cannot run about.

He must be very quiet."

A   Answer each question.

1   Where did Ann go with Blot?
2   What did Blot cut his leg on?
3   What did Ann get for her mother?
4   To what did mother tie Blot?

B   Write *one* word to finish each sentence.

1   "You . . ."
2   "Stop, Blot, ..."
3   "I will carry you . . . ."

C   Write the words in each line that have the *last two letters* like the word in the box.

p**et**	set	sit	let	stop	get
top	shop	tip	dog	blot	hop
d**ay**	way	toy	say	sad	peg

ill	bat	nut
hill	that	cut
will	bag	but
fill	rag	shut

Blot and Ann go for a walk

Blot was shut up for six days but after that his cut was better.

Mother took the rag off his leg, and let him go out with Ann.

"Bow, wow, bow, wow," barked Blot.
"I'm glad I'm not ill any more.
I will chase the ball when you hit it with the bat.
I will run up and down the hill."

"Silly Blot," said Ann. "Stop that and come with me.
I want you to help me fill this bag with nuts."

"Bow, wow," barked Blot.
"I'm coming to help you fill the bag with nuts."

13 A Write each sentence, putting in the missing word:

1 Blot was . . . . up for six days.

2 Mother took the . . . off his leg.

3 Blot was glad he was not . . . any more.

4 Blot ran up and down the . . . .

B Draw a ball, a bat, a bag, a hill.

Write the name under each picture.

C 1 I have four legs. I bark. What am I?

2 I am high. People climb me. My first letter is 'h'.
What am I?

rub	sit	yes
tub	bit	yet
dust	dig	pen
fog	pig	open

The pig and the mouse

Once there was a pig who lived in a pen at a farm.

He had a tub to eat from and yet he was not happy.

"Yes, I know," he said, "I will dig a hole
under my pen."

He made a lot of dust, but no one saw him.

He put his nose deep into the hole.

Then a little mouse bit his nose.

"Ow," said Pig, as he began to rub his nose.

"Go away, Mouse."

"No," said Mouse. "You sit down here in your pen.
If you go out through the open hole
you will get lost in the fog."

A Find the answer and then draw it.

1 I live in a pen. I eat from a tub. A mouse bit my nose. Who am I?

2 I am little. I bit a pig's nose. I told him to sit in his pen. Who am I?

B Write 'Yes' or 'No'.

1 Can a pig fly?

2 Did the pig get out of his pen?

3 Was the pig happy?

4 Is a mouse little?

C Draw a pig in a pen.

Draw a dog in a tub.

look	kill	cap
book	till	tap
took	mill	clap
cook	still	trap

The cook and the mice

Bob threw down his cap.

"It is still raining," he said to his mother.
"Please read me a story till the rain stops.
Look, here is a good book.
Please read to me about the Cook and the Mice."

Mother took the book:

"Once there was a cook who had many mice
in his shop.

They ate all the flour that he got from the mill.

He could not trap them.

His dog would not kill them.

The cook would clap his hands or his foot
and the mice would run away,
but before long they would all be back.

What could the poor cook do?"

A What are these three pictures? Write the correct word on your paper.

bag	mouse	hill
book	trap	mill
cook	cook	till

B Write the words in each line that have the *last two letters* like the one in the box.

cap	tap	took	clap	shop	trap
cook	book	back	took	foot	look
hot	not	that	got	lot	hat

C Here are four words—kill, still, mill, till.
Write each sentence, using one of these words.
1 The cook got his flour from the . . . .
2 His dog would not . . . . the mice.
3 "It is . . . . . raining," said Bob.
4 "Please read me a story . . . . it stops."

all   men   here
ball   ten   where
fall   then   there
small   when   egg

The lost ball

One day Tim and Jess were playing ball.

"Here, catch this, Jess," Tim said, when he threw
the ball high in the air.

But the ball did not fall down so they looked all around.

"Where is it?" cried Tim.

"It went into the tree, but I didn't see it fall," said Jess.

"It must be up there in the tree."

"We will ask the men who are painting the house
to look for it in the tree," said Tim.

Then where do you think they found the ball?

It was in a bird's nest with ten small eggs
and not one egg was broken.

19 A   Make a picture. Put in it:
a tree   a nest in the tree   the eggs in the nest
a ball in the nest   the man on a ladder

B   Can you find *five* words in the story which end with
the letters *-en*? Write the words on your paper.

C   Write the answers to these questions:
1   Where did the ball fall?
2   What were the men painting?
3   How many eggs were there in the nest?
4   Were they big or small eggs?

end	sing	good
send	king	wood
mend	thing	foot
lend	them	boot

The king who was lost

One day a king lost his way in the woods.

It grew dark.

He began to call and sing, but no one heard him.

In the dark he fell over a piece of wood,
and tore his boot.

He took off the boot and his sock and walked
with one bare foot.

At the end of the road he saw a farmer.

The farmer did not know that he was a king,
but he took him home.

"I will mend your boot and lend you a horse."

"How good these people are," thought the king.
"I shall send them many good things when I return."

A   Write the sentences that are true:
1   The king fell over a piece of wood.
2   The king hurt his foot.
3   The king saw a farmer at the end of the road.
4   The farmer said, "I will not mend your boot."

B   Write *three* words that rhyme with *ring*.
Write *three* words that rhyme with *lend*.

C   Draw the king with his boot in his hand.

D   Write a letter from the king to the farmer
to thank him for mending his boot.
Say at the end of the letter,
"I am sending you many good things."

ring	old	call
bring	hold	tall
spring	told	wall
gold	bold	calling

Springtime in Switzerland

Peter and Marie live in Switzerland.

In spring they help their father bring the cows
out of the barn where they have been all the winter.

"Marie, Marie." It was Peter calling Marie
to hold two cows.

"Now," said Peter, "we will have to tie each cow
to a ring in the wall."

He told Marie to tie her two cows and then
to call the others.

Every cow knew its name.

The tall one, the small one, the white one,
the gold one, the young one, the old one—
each had a name, and each came out of the barn
with bold steps, to Marie.

A Write each word. Then write it with *-ing* at the end.

1 call — calling   4 hold —
2 bring —   5 ring —
3 sing —   6 send —

B Read the story again. Write the words left out:

1 One cow was *tall*.   4 One cow was . . .
2 One cow was . . .   5 One cow was . . .
3 One cow was . . .   6 One cow was . . .

C Write each sentence, putting in the missing word:

1 In . . . Father brings the cows out of the barn.
2 Peter told Marie to . . . two cows.
3 Marie tied the cows to the . . . in the . . .

him	was	her
his	wash	she
this	want	they
sum	drum	what

After school

Jack and Jess have come home from school.

"I have two sums to do," said Jack.

"What have you to do, Jess?"

"Oh, I have only one sum," said Jess.

"We will do our sums," said Jack, "then I want to play.
I have a new drum and a gun."

So they did their homework.

Jess did her sum and was soon ready to play.

"Now I will wash this drum and make it shine,"
said Jess.

So while Jack was doing his sums
she washed the drum.

Then Jess said to him, "Can you see what a good shine
I have given it?"

$$24$$
$$22+$$
———

$$34$$
$$\times 3$$
———

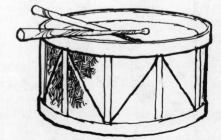

A   Write the sentences that are true:
1   "I have four sums to do," said Jack.
2   "I have a new drum," said Jack.
3   "We will not do our sums," said Jack.
4   Jess said, "Now I will wash this drum."

B   Here are three words: shines, want, washed.
Write each sentence using *one* of these words.
1   "I . . . to play," said Jack.
2   Jess . . . the drum.
3   "Can you see how the drum . . . ?" said Jess.

C   Write the words in the list at the top of the story
under their right letter:

d	h	s	t	w

see	six	by
tree	fix	cry
been	box	try
sweet	fox	sky

The fox and the grapes

One day when the sky was blue
Mr Fox went for a walk.

He had not been out long
when he came to a tree by a wall.

Hanging over the wall were some sweet grapes.

"What is this I see?" said Mr Fox. "I will try
to get some grapes."

He ran six steps and with a loud cry he jumped high
in the air.

Try, try, try, he could not get the grapes.

"I'll fix this," said Mr Fox. "I'll get a box."

But still he could not get the grapes.
So Mr Fox walked away.

"Those grapes are not sweet," he said.
"They are sour."

A   Answer these questions with 'Yes' or 'No'.
1   Was the sky red?
2   Were the grapes hanging over the wall?
3   Did Mr Fox take eight steps?
4   Can a fox jump?
5   Did the fox get the grapes?

B   Write *three* words that have *ee* in them.
Can you think of two more like them?

C   Draw: the wall, the tree, the grapes,
the fox on the box.
Write the name under each picture.

name	our	wish
came	out	dish
game	about	fish
same	you	your

A party game

I will tell you about a new game we played
with the boys and girls who came to our last party.

You can try the same game at your next party.

The name of the game is Kim's Game.

Put a lot of little things on a tray or on a dish.

Put on anything you wish, like a small book,
a tin, a pin, a pen, a ball, a ring, and so on.

Bring out the tray of things and show it to everyone
for a little while.

Then take it away and see how many things
each boy or girl can remember.

A   Write the names of six things that you could put on the tray.

B   Write the sentences and put a word in each space.
These words will help you: party, game, things.
1   Boys and girls came to the . . .
2   The name of the . . . is Kim's Game.
3   Little . . . only are put on the tray.

C   Write all the words you know that end with the letters -ish.
Write all the words you know that end with the letters -ame.
Write three words with the letters ou in them.

ink	eat	take
drink	sea	cake
milk	read	make
rich	much	made

A picnic by the sea

Last week we went for a picnic by the sea.

Mother said to Jess and me, "Pack the basket with things to eat and drink.

Don't put in too much or you will make the basket too heavy to carry."

We put in milk to drink and Mother made us a rich cake to take.

Father took some books to read.

I took my fishing line.

Mother took a pen and ink to write letters.

We all had a fine time.

At the end of the day we got a train home.

We were all tired but happy.

A Write *one* word to answer each question.

1 Where did they go for the picnic?
2 What did they drink?
3 What did Mother make?
4 What did Father take?

B Write the words that rhyme *in pairs*,
like *seat, meat:*

seat hill sink made try
pink meat pill sky spade

C Draw a bottle of milk, a bottle of ink,
a rich cake, the sea with a ship on it,
a book, a basket.
Write the name under each picture.

God	far	put
soft	car	pull
from	cart	full
doll	clean	part

Straw men

One day two boys from our class at school
went far out into the country.

They went to pull home a cart full of clean, soft straw
from a farm in the country.

They put part of the straw in a basket
and took it to school.

They gave some straw to everyone
to make straw toys.

One boy made a straw man with arms and legs
by tying it with string.

One girl made a small, straw doll.

She used blue ribbon to tie the straw.

The doll looked fine when she sat it up in a toy car.

A Write the sentences, using *one* of the words in bold.

1 The boys went to a **far   farm.**

2 They went to **pull   put**   home a cart full of straw
from the farm.

3 The doll sat up in a toy **car   cart.**

B Write -*ing* on to these words:

cart   clean   pull   look   part
fill   say   hold   find   cry

C 1   What did one boy make with his straw?

2   What did one girl make with her straw?

3   What else could you make with soft straw?

hand	jam	long
sand	jar	song
land	jump	for
stand	morning	are

Monkey and crocodile

"Good morning, Croc," said Monkey to Crocodile
who lay on the warm sand.
"I see you are on the land."

"Yes," said Croc.
"I have been in the water for a long time.
You can sing me a song to send me to sleep,
Monkey."

"Oh, I can't sing," said Monkey, "but I can stand
on my hands and I can jump."

"Oh, that's no use to me," said Croc.
"Get me something to eat.
Get me a jar of sweet jam.

Then I will let you pick my teeth," said Croc,
"and you can tell your friends how brave you are."

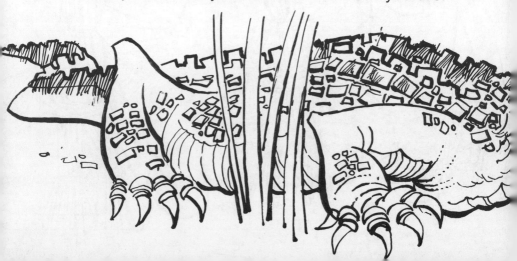

A 1 Write *three* words that rhyme with *stand*.
2 Write *two* words that start with *ja*.

B Write the missing word on your paper:
1 "Good . . ., Croc," said Monkey.
2 Croc lay on the warm . . .
3 "I see you are on the . . ."

C Answer 'Yes' or 'No'.
1 Had Crocodile been in the water?
2 Did Monkey sing a song?
3 Can a crocodile sing?
4 Can a monkey stand on his hands?
5 Can a crocodile go on the land?

nest	**ship**	**say**
best	**slip**	**day**
rest	**skip**	**today**
saw	**help**	**play**

The best game

One day we saw six children at play.

"Today," said Bob, "we will play three games.
Then we will say which one we like the best."

"Let us play that we are on a ship," said Jack.
"Tom, you can help me to steer the ship."

"As we have nothing to do," said Jill and Jess,
"we will rest like birds in a nest."

After a little while the girls said,
"Let us skip."

So everyone had to skip.

Then Tom cried, "Now for a game of 'slip and slide'."

The girls liked skipping best.

The boys liked 'slip and slide' best.

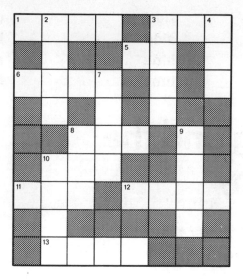

Put the missing words in the puzzle.

Across

1 "Let us play that we are on a . . ."
3 One . . . we saw six children at play.
5 "We have nothing . . . do," said Jill.
6 "Now for a game of '. . . and slide'," said Tom.
8 One day we . . . six children at play.
10 "We will . . . which game we like best."
11 Birds fly in the . . .
12 "We will . . . like birds in a nest."
13 Bob said, "We will . . . three games."

Down

2 "You can . . . me steer the ship."
3 A girl likes to play with a . . .
4 "Tom, . . . can help me steer the ship."
7 "Today we will . . . three games," said Bob.
8 "We will . . . which one we like best."
9 The girls liked skipping . . .
10 The girls said, "Let us . . ."

age	ride	deep
cage	side	keep
page	hide	sleep
into	time	feet

The king and the page boy

One cold night in winter time, a king saw
a man of great age in the snow.

He called his page to his side and asked him
about the old man.

"He is very poor and he lives in a hut in the forest.
His only friend is a bird in a cage," said the page.

"We will not sleep to-night," said the king,
"until we take some food to his hut."

So the king and the page set out to walk, not ride,
to his hut.

The snow came to hide the moon.

The page was tired and cold.
"Keep close to me," said the king,
"and put your feet deep into my steps."

"Oh, how warm your foot-steps are," said the page.
"I can go on now."

A Write the words in each line that have the *last three letters* like the one in the box.

rage	age	way	page	cage	came
tide	ride	rid	side	said	hide
sl**eep**	feet	deep	keep	feed	peep

B Write *one* word to answer each question.
1 Who did the king call to his side?
2 What was the old man's only friend?
3 What came to hide the moon?

C Write six words that have four letters each.
Write six words that have five letters each.
Write four words that end in the letters *and*.

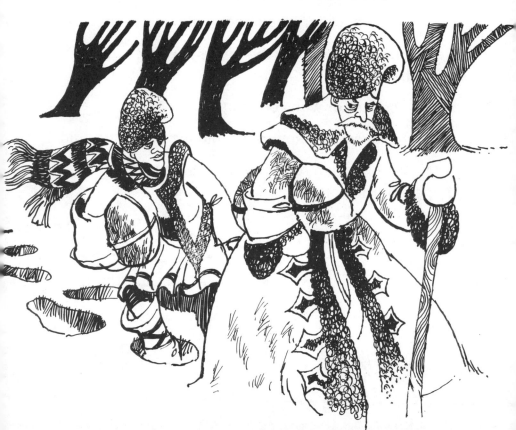

bite	may	ever
white	way	every
like	away	never
	stay	very

The white rabbit

Once there was a white rabbit who lived near a farm.

Every night he went to the farm for some turnips.

He could not stay away for very long.

He would say to himself, "I like turnips so much
I could eat them for ever and ever.
I may never get any more turnips.
I must go back for just another bite."

And so he would soon be on his way back again
to the farm.

But the farmer was very angry.

"I will take all these turnips into the barn," he said.

Next night when rabbit came there was
not a turnip left.

41 A 1 I am white. I live near a farm. I like turnips.
Who am I?
2 I grow on a farm. A white rabbit took a bite out
of me. A farmer took me into the barn. Who am I?

B Write each sentence, putting in the missing word:
very, every, ever, never.
1 The rabbit went to the farm . . . night.
2 He was . . . fond of eating turnips.
3 He could eat them for . . . and ever.
4 "I must go back for another bite," he said,
"because I may . . . get any more turnips."

coat	went	ice
boat	sent	nice
road	bent	drop
with	sell	bend

The ice boat

One day it was so cold that every pond and river froze hard.

The ice was so thick that you could walk on it like a road.

It would not break or bend.

When Tom and Bob went out to play they each put on a thick coat.

"Let's make an ice boat," said Tom.

"For an ice boat we want a box with wheels. The grocer will sell us a nice box."

Then they put four wheels on it.

One wheel was bent a little but it still went round.

Next they put up a pole and a sail and the wind sent them along over the ice.

A   Use *one* word to answer each question.
1   What did Tom and Bob wear?
2   What did they make?
3   What did the grocer sell them?
4   What sent them over the ice?

B   Write down all the words in this story that end with *ent*.

C   Write three new words by putting *m, n,* and *r* in front of *ice*.

D   Write three more words that end with *ell*.

head	**mine**	**room**
bread	**line**	**moon**
lost	**nine**	**soon**
school	**five**	**have**

My school

I go to a tiny school.

It is just one room and we have only nine children in the school.

There will soon be fourteen children when five more come from another farm.

My two brothers and two sisters and I each ride a pony to school.

We ride along in a line.

I am the oldest, so I ride mine at the head of the line.

We have bread, meat and fruit for our lunch.

It is very late when we get home.

One day we were so late that the moon had risen.

Our parents thought we were lost.

A   Write the words that go together:

school	jar
jam	nest
bird's	moon
full	room
bird	ball
foot	cage

B   What do the children have for lunch?

C   Draw the school. Draw nine children in it.

D   Write the words in each line that have the *last three letters* like the one in the box.

d**ine**	mine	mind	nine	moon	line
m**oon**	room	soon	home	come	noon
l**ost**	late	cost	coat	most	post

pay	rope	cup
bay	hope	pup
hay	hole	under
lay	pole	said

Hay time

"I hope to gather the hay today," said my father.
"Are you coming, too?"

"Oh, yes, please," I cried.
"May I bring my pup with me?"

"Well, yes," said Father, "but bring a piece of rope
and tie him up.

I cannot pay my men to play with a pup," he said
with a laugh.

We tied my pup to a pole near the edge of the field.

He dug a hole and lay in it, asleep.

We were all very happy.

During the morning we stopped to have a cup of tea.

A   Write each sentence, putting in the missing word.
1   "I hope to gather the . . ."
2   "Bring a piece of . . ."
3   "I cannot . . . my men to play with a . . ."
4   The pup dug a . . .

B   Write four words, one to rhyme with each
of these words: rope   pole   bay   pup

C   Draw a picture and put in it:
the pup, the pole, the rope, the hay, the hole.
Write the names under the picture.

pipe	feed	now
wipe	need	cow
ripe	sheep	how
were	paper	down

On the farm

I live on a farm. We have some cows and sheep and pigs.

I have a cow of my own.

Now I know how to feed her and what she needs to make her give a lot of milk.

Her name is Snowdrop.

She is as white as paper.

I wipe her coat to make it shine.

One day, when all the cows were in the yard, I found Snowdrop lying down.

She was ill from eating ripe berries.

"Oh, Father, Snowdrop is ill," I cried.

Father poured some oil down a pipe into her mouth.

She was better in a few days.

A Write these sentences, filling in the spaces.
These words will help you: paper, cow, were.
1 I have a . . . of my own.
2 She is as white as . . .
3 All the cows . . . in the yard.

B Here are two lines of words. Each of the words in
the first line rhymes with a word in the second line,
like this: ripe — wipe.
See if you can put the others in pairs.

ripe   feed   town   now   keep
need   down   how   wipe   sheep

C Write the names of three animals on the farm.

boy	gave	round
toy	give	ground
flag	live	round
count	hall	mouth

Tony, the clever seal

One day another boy and I went to the Zoo.

We first went into a large hall to see the parrots.

One parrot held a toy flag in his foot.

Then we found the lions and saw the men
give them their meat.

"Come, let us see the monkeys now," I said.

After going almost all round the ground
we came to the seals.

They live on fish.

One seal, Tony, would jump in the air and catch fish
in his mouth when the keeper gave them to him.

When the keeper said, "Count, Tony," he would nod
his head five times.

A Write out the words in each line that have the *last two letters* like the one in the box.

joy	zoo	boy	Tony	toy	day
fi**ve**	give	flag	live	lions	dive
bou**nd**	round	mouth	found	ground	

B Find two little words in each big word.
Write them like this: sunrise; sun, rise.
downstairs   football   flagpole   lifeboat
cowshed   breadboard   moonrise   sunset

C Write each sentence with its right ending.
These words will help you: fish, corn, meat, bones.
1 Lions like . . .   3 Seals like . . .
2 Parrots like . . .   4 Dogs like . . .

rain	find	home
train	kind	nose
again	wind	rose
going	doing	raining

The wind and the rain

Last winter we had a lot of wind and rain.

One day it was raining so hard that I could not catch the train to school.

"You had better stay at home, today," said Mother.

Another morning as I went to school I saw something under a rose-bush.

I was surprised to find a poor little puppy.

It was wet from nose to tail.

I did not know where it was going or what it was doing; but it looked up at me as much as to say, "Please be kind to me. Please take me home."

So I went home and gave him to my mother, who dried him and made him warm again.

A   Make new words by writing *-ing* on to these words:

rain   go   do   find   see   throw   catch   stay

B   Answer these questions:
1   Why did you not catch the train to school?
2   What did Mother say?
3   What was under a rose-bush?
4   What did Mother do with the puppy?

C   Write each sentence with its correct ending.
These words will help you: milk, grass, rain, hay.
1   Sheep like . . .   3   Cats like . . .
2   Ducks like . . .   4   Cows like . . .

other	father	ate
mother	winter	late
brother	summer	gate
sister	able	table

Summer or winter?

"Hurrah for summer time," shouted Jill, as she came through the garden gate.

"I like the hot days in summer."

"Yes," said Mother. "I like the summer best, too. It is light so late that we are able to stay longer in the garden."

"Oh, I like winter best," said my brother and my other sister.

"You can get warm by the fire as you sit round the table and read."

"Well," said Father, "I like both winter and summer."

"Mew, mew," said Ritsie, our cat, as she ate a bone. "I agree with you, Father."

A Write the answers on your paper.

1 Who likes the summer best?

2 Who likes the winter best?

3 Who likes summer and winter?

B 1 Write the sentence that tells why Mother likes the summer best.

2 Write the sentence that tells why my brother and my other sister like the winter best.

C Write the *two* correct words on your paper:

What can Mother do? fly wash clap

What can Father do? count crow read

What can a calf do? sleep talk bite

dinner	back	fly
supper	black	dry
butter	sick	seven
water	bill	duck

Little black duck

One night as we sat having our supper at about seven o'clock we heard a very faint quack at the back door.

When we opened the door we saw a little black duck that looked very sick.

He could not stand up and he could not fly.

We put him in a warm, dry box.

Father said, "Pour a little milk down his bill."

We did this and then he went to sleep.

Next day my brother and I fed him with bread and butter for his dinner.

He liked this very much.

Then he had a drink of water.

A 1 Who was at the back door?

2 Where did he sleep?

3 What did he have for his dinner?

4 What did he drink?

B Write the words that go together, like *cat* and *kitten*.

bread   sister

brother   butter

mother   calf

cow   pepper

salt   father

C Draw the black duck in a box.
Draw the jug of milk.

D Write three words that end in *-er*.

58

snow	kitten	sorry
blow	letter	funny
grow	lesson	sunny
show	little	happy

Ritsie and her kittens

We call our cat Ritsie.

She has a snow white coat and four little kittens.

There are three black and white kittens
and a light grey one.

Ritsie is very happy with her family and likes
to show them off.

It is a lesson to us all to see how cleverly
she carries them, as lightly as a letter.

I will be sorry when they grow up because they are
so funny playing with their mother's tail.

When it is sunny I take them out on the grass to play.

When the cold winds blow they stay inside.

A Write the sentences that are true:
1 Our cat has five little kittens.
2 One kitten is light grey.
3 When the cold winds blow, I take them out on the grass to play.
4 The kittens play with their mother's tail.

B Write the correct words on your paper:
1 What can a kitten do?   bark   play   read
2 Ritsie's coat is   white   black   brown
3 Ritsie is very   sad   happy   old

C Write these words. Then write them with -ing on the end of each word.
snow   blow   grow   fly   find

arm	girl	one
hard	bird	love
dark	first	come
making	river	coming

Whiskers

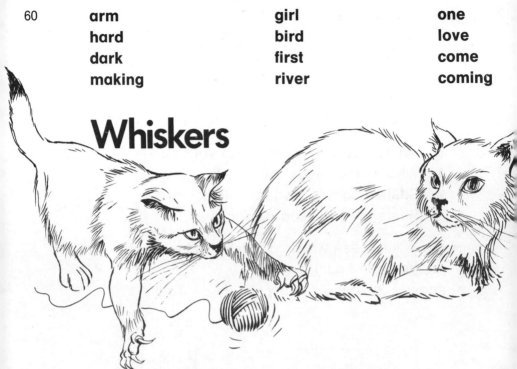

I gave the kittens away to my girl friends,
but we kept one of Ritsie's first kittens.

We kept her first son and I called him Whiskers
because he has such long whiskers.

I love to see Whiskers trying hard to catch a bird.

He creeps along, not making a sound,
but the birds always fly away.

When I am coming home from school,
Ritsie or Whiskers will sometimes come
to meet me.

If I go for a walk to the river they will come too,
even if it's dark.

Whiskers still likes me to hold him in my arms.

A I have long whiskers. I can see in the dark.
I like to catch birds. Who am I?

B Write three words in each column:

3 letters	4 letters	5 letters	6 letters

C Put the right words in each sentence:
come, making, one, coming, first
1 We kept . . . of Ritsie's . . . kittens.
2 When I am . . . home from school, Ritsie will . . . to meet me.
3 Whiskers creeps along, not . . . a sound.

spoke	hair	pretty
smoke	chair	dress
fire	fair	grass
baby	story	fairy

The Christmas tree 1

Nancy said to her mother,
"Please tell us a fairy story."

Nancy sat in front of the fire minding the baby.

Mother moved her chair away from the smoke
of the fire.

She spoke softly so that the baby would go to sleep.

"I shall tell you a fairy story about a Christmas Fairy,"
Mother began.

"In the room of a house stood a pretty Christmas tree.

Only Mother and the Christmas Fairy
knew the tree was there.

The Christmas Fairy, with her fair hair
and her pretty grass dress, knew,
because she peeped in the window."

A   Write the sentences that are true.
1   Mother did not tell a fairy story.
2   Nancy was minding the baby.
3   The fairy had fair hair.
4   The fairy had a pretty grass dress.

B Write out the words in each line which have the *last three letters* like the one in the box.

spoke	stroke	smoke	story	spoke	chair
fairy	pretty	fairy	hair	fair	hairy
fire	front	softly	fire	hair	tire

C Draw a Christmas tree. Put on it:
a toy gun, a rag doll, a red tin money box, a bag of nuts,
a small ball, a bat, a drum.

fast	sold	penny
last	cold	add
each	colder	apple
over	only	after

The Christmas tree 2

"Were they the only ones that knew?" said Nancy.

"Well, the man who sold the Christmas tree knew.

And the lady who sold Mother the little bags,
with an apple in each, for a penny, knew too.

Tom, the cat, knew too, when he ran fast into the room
after Mother.

Mr and Mrs Mouse were the last to see it.

They saw it when they ran over the floor, very quickly,
as it was getting colder and colder."

"Well, now, let me add up," said Nancy,
"to see how many knew about the Christmas tree.
Mother, the Fairy, the man, the lady, the cat,
Mr and Mrs Mouse. That's seven."

A   Answer these questions:
1   What did the man sell to Mother?
2   What did the lady sell to Mother?
3   Who were the last to find the tree?
4   How many knew about it altogether?

B   Write these words:
fast,   cold,   slow,   fair.
Now write each word again with -er on the end of it.
Write six other words that end in -er.

C   Write the word that means more than one:

one	more than one
penny	pennies
fairy	
apple	
tree	
mouse	
man	
dress	
chair	

ear	talk	house
hear	walk	mouse
dear	horse	than
year	near	ask

The Christmas tree 3

 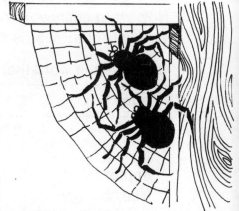

Now that night, when all was still in the house,
the little grey spiders could hear
Mr and Mrs Mouse talking.

"My dear," said Mr Mouse, "I will talk softly
into your ear so that the spiders won't hear."

But the spiders were very near and they did hear.

"We must see the Christmas tree this year, too,"
said Mr Spider.

"We want to see it more than anything else.

When the Christmas Fairy comes on her fairy horse,
I will walk over and talk to her.
I will ask her if we can see the Christmas tree."

The Christmas Fairy came.

A   Write out the words in each line that end like the one in the box.

sp**oke**	stroke smoke story spoke chair
f**airy**	pretty fairy hair fair hairy
f**ire**	front softly fire hair tire

B   Draw a horse, a house, and a mouse.
Write the name under each picture.

C   Put these words in the correct place:
ear, hear, year. Write each sentence.
1   "I will talk softly into your . . .
so that the spiders won't . . .," said Mr Mouse.
2   "We must see the Christmas tree this . . .,"
said Mr Spider.

face	eye	more
race	eyes	store
left	tail	plant
wait	miss	lady

The Christmas tree 4

Mr Spider left his dark corner and looked up into her face with sad eyes.

"Dear Miss Fairy Lady, we do want to see the Christmas tree."

The Fairy Lady, with a twinkle in her eye, said, "Mr Spider, wait until the night before Christmas. Then you can see it."

That night all the spiders came out.

They raced all over the tree, from twig to twig.

There were cobwebs all over it, like the dew on a plant.

Every twig had a thin, silver tail or cobweb.

"Oh," said the Fairy, when she saw it, "I will change all the cobwebs into gold."

Next morning the children said, "Oh, how beautiful — a Christmas tree with shining golden cobwebs on it."

A   Put *-ing* on the end of these words, to make new words: talk, walk, ask, hear, draw.

B   Write the answers to these questions:
1   Did the spiders come out at night or in the day time?
2   What did the spiders leave on the tree?
3   What did the fairy do to the tree?
4   What did the children say in the morning?

C   Write words to rhyme with these words:
more, race, tail, tree.

Notes for the teacher

The *Essential Read-Spell Books* provide a new and combined approach to the teaching of both spelling and reading. They are useful for pupils in junior and middle schools, and for older pupils who gain satisfaction from more practice material.

This method is based on research findings that in all aspects of language teaching we should:
a   use as many forms of presentation as possible;
b   integrate methods of presentation;
c   make all material as meaningful as possible to pupils.

Thus the *Essential Read-Spell Books* employ a combined spelling-reading-writing method. This enables children to gain:
a   *maximum efficiency in spelling* words by writing them and by understanding their meaning in prose and through written exercises;
b   *additional practice in reading* by use of graded material to consolidate both spelling and reading.

Procedure

First Step   Words are learnt in groups of similar structure.

Second Step   This first learning of words is consolidated by reading them in specially prepared short stories or prose.

Third Step   Both *spelling and reading* (of harder words) are *strengthened through written exercises*, which emphasise *structure* and *meaning* and help pupils with *comprehension*.

Suggestions for class use

(Full suggestions for class procedure are given in *The Teachers' Book*.)

These suggestions vary according to the calibre of the class, and are based on three 30-minute lessons per week.

First Lesson   Six words are studied for spelling (with retarded children this may be 3 or 4 words only). Words are learnt by looking at-saying-tracing-writing them. The prose is read. Words are tested.

Second Lesson   Six more words are studied. The prose is read again. Words are tested.

Third Lesson   Exercises are worked from the prose.

Of course, many teachers will wish to make variations in the above.

The material may be used for individual, group or class work. The main principle is to see that spelling, reading and writing are blended in a natural way to the advantage of the pupil.

The authors would like to thank Miss J. Thompson for help with the manuscript and proofs.

Thomas Nelson and Sons Ltd
Nelson House   Mayfield Road
Walton-on-Thames   Surrey
KT12 5PL   UK

51 York Place
Edinburgh
EH1 3JD   UK

Thomas Nelson (Hong Kong) Ltd
Toppan Building 10/F
22A Westlands Road
Quarry Bay   Hong Kong

Thomas Nelson Australia
102 Dodds Street
South Melbourne
Victoria 3205   Australia

Nelson Canada
1120 Birchmount Road
Scarborough   Ontario
M1K 5G4   Canada

First published by Macmillan Education Ltd 1961

This edition published by Thomas Nelson and Sons Ltd 1992

ISBN 0-17-424497-5
NPN 9 8 7 6 5 4 3

Printed in Hong Kong